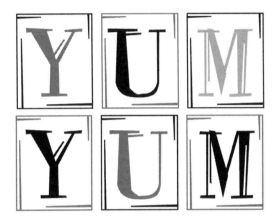

FABULOUS FOODS
AT HOME

Lynn Rollins

Copyright © 2009 Lynn Rollins
All rights reserved.

ISBN: 1-4392-6592-5
ISBN-13: 9781439265925

ABOUT ME

As a little girl, I would painstakingly make the *most* elaborate mud pies you've ever imagined. I would name them with delectable titles that sounded so real, my mother would leave her post in the garden next to me where she was working and would literally *run* to the kitchen to try and recreate what I had just invented with dirt, flowers, little pebbles, grass clippings, and whatever else the lush gardens we had offered me as "ingredients."

Julia Child was my choice on TV, not the popular kids' shows. Julia held my rapt attention. I was preparing French cuisine by the age of twelve. Catering often through high school and college, my love of cooking and making it my chosen profession took hold. After college at everyone's favorite North Carolina school, UNC-Chapel Hill, I dashed off to London to the well-known and respected Cordon Bleu, where I became a "certified" chef.

After the Cordon Bleu, I became a chef at the long-standing gourmet-to-go shop in Richmond, Virginia, Gourmet Delights. I spent five years in Richmond and had the privilege to serve as the head chef at the Catlin Abbott House and the Carrington Row Inn. I also did private catering for the Virginia Museum and other highly esteemed clients.

ABOUT ME

I returned to my childhood hometown of Chapel Hill to become the head chef at A Southern Season. It was a wonderful experience and a springboard to opening my own catering business, The Lane, which has grown and prospered since 1988.

After purchasing a home in Blowing Rock over three years ago, I found myself spending more and more time in the mountains. I maintain a lovely home in Chapel Hill, but I can count on my fingers and toes the number of nights I spend there a year. I love being in the mountains and decided there needed to be a store where people could pick up fresh, homemade foods to make their lives a little easier. I take no shortcuts and use only fresh vegetables and fruits, which, in the summer, come from Yum Gardens, a two-acre garden I plant and maintain near the shop.

In this, my fiftieth year, I wanted to do something memorable. I have always wanted to do a cookbook, and I thought, how fitting to remember writing it in this important milestone of a year. I'm celebrating my love for cooking and a big birthday all at once! Thank you for sharing this special year with me!

ABOUT YUM YUM

In the summer of 2008, I opened Yum Yum, a gourmet take-out shop in the mountains of North Carolina. In every other town I've lived in or visited, there are several take-out shops. There were none in the town in which I opened. Because of the generations of people who summer here, I knew it would be a huge success. The phone started ringing while I was still renovating the space. Word had gotten out that good food was coming soon! We were taking orders and we weren't even open yet.

I had the great fortune to have two students from UNC-Chapel Hill who had helped me in previous years in Chapel Hill and were willing to come to the mountains for the summer to help me get up and running. The familiarity of being with people you've worked with before is invaluable. Jack and Alex were wonderful!

ABOUT YUM YUM

Jack Garvey (left) and Alex Gillon (right)

You know, you hear about doing what you love for a living. I do exactly what I love every single day, and I appreciate all of the pieces that have fallen so perfectly into place to make it happen. I hope if you find yourself in the mountains, you'll come visit us! We'd love to have you!

Yum Yum Fabulous Foods To Go
9872 N.C. 105 South
Banner Elk, N.C. 28604
828-963-6100

LITTLE BITES

CHEESE SNAPS

12 ounces shredded parmesan

Heat a nonstick skillet over medium-high heat. Sprinkle parmesan into 2-to-3-inch-round shapes until all cheese is used. Keep them light so they look lacy. When golden on underside, remove from pan and place on cooling racks. They should be completely crispy.

Serves 4

DOO DAH DATES

4 ¼ cups all-purpose flour

1 pound grated extra-sharp cheddar cheese

1 pound chilled butter

1 teaspoon salt

¼ teaspoon cayenne pepper

1 cup chopped pecans

1 cup chopped dates

In a Cuisinart, process flour and cheddar until cheddar is like meal. Add butter, salt, cayenne, and process until blended. With hands, mix in nuts and dates. Roll into 1-inch balls and flatten on buttered cookie sheets. Bake at 350 degrees for 15-20 minutes until lightly browned and crisp.

Makes 100

CORNCAKES

One of my favorite dinners is North Carolina Barbecue, Oriental Coleslaw, Pineapple Baked Beans, and these fabulous little Corncakes.

1 package Jiffy Cornbread Mix
1 egg
2 tablespoons melted butter
¾ cup whole milk
1 cup white corn
Salt and pepper

In a medium bowl, blend all ingredients lightly. Spoon tiny cakes, the size of a quarter, onto a hot buttered griddle. Cook until golden brown on both sides. Serve with pepper jelly and sour cream.

Serves 12

BRANDIED FRUIT MASCARPONE

12 ounces cream cheese

½ cup butter

½ cup sour cream

½ cup sugar

1 package unflavored gelatin

¼ cup cold water

1 cup toasted, slivered almonds

1 cup golden raisins

Brandy

Grated rind of 2 lemons

In a Cuisinart, mix cream cheese, butter, sour cream, and sugar. Soften gelatin in ¼ cup cold water. Mix almonds and raisins in bowl. Add enough brandy to soak for 30 minutes. Drain. Mix gelatin with cream cheese mixture. Fold in nuts, raisins, and lemon rind. Spoon into greased 1-quart mold. Chill and release. Serve with red grapes and McVitie's Digestives or Trader Joe's Triple Gingersnaps.

Serves 30

CRANBERRY RELISH BUTTER

This makes a terrific Christmas gift!

½ cup butter
1½ cups confectioners' sugar
1 tablespoon fresh lemon juice
Grated rind of 2 oranges
1 cup cooked, drained, and cooled cranberries

In a Cuisinart, blend butter, sugar, juice, and orange rind. Add cranberries and pulse until blended in but not pureed. Berries will be slightly chunky. Serve with McVitie's Digestives or Trader Joe's Triple Gingersnaps.

Serves 20

HUMMUS

4 cups cooked and drained chickpeas

½ cup tahini (sesame paste)

⅓ cup olive oil

Juice of 2-3 lemons

4 minced cloves garlic

2 teaspoons cumin

Pinch of salt

Pinch of fresh black pepper

In a Cuisinart, combine all ingredients. Process until completely smooth. Taste and correct seasoning with additional lemon juice, salt, and pepper. Store in refrigerator. Serve with hot buttered pita.

Makes 1 quart

DILL DIP

The quintessential dip for crudite!

1 cup sour cream
1 cup Duke's mayonnaise
2 tablespoons chopped fresh parsley
2 teaspoons grated Vidalia
2 teaspoons dried dill
2 teaspoons Jane's Krazy Mixed-Up Salt
1 teaspoon fresh lemon juice

In a small bowl, mix all of the ingredients and chill.

Serves 20

ELEANOR'S HOT CHEESE DIP

This is my mother's recipe. We were eating nacho dip in the '60s before it was cool to eat nacho dip. This is the real thing! We always had it with Fritos. Use the corn chip of your choice.

1 large chopped Vidalia

1 tablespoon butter

1½ cups drained petite diced tomatoes

4 ounces green chilies (or jalapenos if you like heat!)

¼ teaspoon chili powder

1 teaspoon salt

½ teaspoon pepper

1 pound grated extra-sharp cheddar

In a skillet, cook the onions in butter until tender. Add remaining ingredients. Heat thoroughly, but whatever you do, don't boil it! It will break. You may use a bain marie (water bath) to be safe.

Serves 6-8

MUSHROOM GRATIN

1 pound sliced button mushrooms

Butter

2 teaspoons chicken base*

*(concentrated chicken stock in a paste form available at specialty food shops and many grocers)

¼ cup hot water

2 tablespoons all-purpose flour

½ cup cream

Dash of white pepper

½ cup shredded parmesan

Place mushrooms in an 8-inch buttered gratin or other shallow baking dish. In a blender carafe, mix remaining ingredients and blend until smooth. Pour over mushrooms and dot with butter. Bake at 350 degrees for 30 minutes until brown and bubbly. Serve with croutes.*

Serves 8

*To make croutes, have your bakery slice a baguette in ¼ inch slices. On a cookie sheet, place slices of the baguette in a single layer. Bake at 300 degrees for 40-60 minutes, turning slices every 10-15 minutes. They will be slightly golden and completely crisped. Cool and store in a Ziploc.

SAUSAGE AND APPLE STUFFED MUSHROOMS

1 pound cooked, drained, and crumbled Neese's Sage Sausage

1 grated Braeburn apple

2 tablespoons minced Vidalia

1 cup fresh bread crumbs

½ teaspoon dried thyme

½ teaspoon garlic salt

¼ teaspoon fresh black pepper

2 tablespoons chopped fresh parsley

½ cup white wine to deglaze pan

Button mushrooms, stems removed (size will determine how many, 1 pound or more)

In a skillet, mix all ingredients except wine and mushrooms. Sauté until the apple is tender. Add wine and heat until completely absorbed. Stuff each mushroom with mixture and place on a greased cookie sheet. Bake at 350 degrees for 10 minutes.

Serves 8-10

PICKLED SHRIMP

5 pounds peeled, deveined, steamed shrimp

1 large sliced Vidalia

2 cups olive oil

1½ cups cider vinegar

⅓ cup capers

1 sliced lemon

¼ cup chopped fresh parsley

Salt and pepper

4 dashes Tabasco

4 dashes Worcestershire

2 teaspoons Jane's Krazy Mixed-Up Salt

1 teaspoon dried dill

Mix all in a gallon jar with a lid. Chill for 6 hours and shake every hour to coat the shrimp. Drain and serve chilled.

Serves 12

IN A BOWL

FRUIT GAZPACHO

32 ounces apple juice

28 ounces apricot nectar

2 cups pineapple juice

16 ounces sliced and sweetened strawberries

2 peeled and diced apples

2 peeled and diced pears

½ peeled and diced cantaloupe

Additional diced fresh fruit (blueberries, pineapples, apples, pears, raspberries) to stir into puree

Puree juices and fruits. Stir in additional fruit and serve chilled.

Serves 10

COLD CUCUMBER SOUP

On a hot summer's day, using cucumbers right out of the garden, this can be so refreshing garnished with mint leaves.

½ chopped Vidalia

2 tablespoons butter

1 minced clove garlic

3 peeled, seeded, and sliced cucumbers

3 tablespoons all-purpose flour

2 cups chicken stock *see index

Salt and fresh pepper to taste

¾ cup sour cream

In a skillet, cook onion in butter until tender. Add garlic and cucumbers. Cook until tender. Add flour and stir well. Add stock and cook until thickened, 20-30 minutes. Add salt and pepper. Chill 4 hours. Remove and whisk in sour cream before serving.

Serves 4

BUTTERNUT SQUASH AND APPLE SOUP

I am so fortunate to have two acres on which there are many apple trees. The cool nights and warm days of the mountains grow the best apples ever. The Rome and McIntosh are wonderful in this soup. I'd also use a Winesap or Braeburn from the grocers. A helpful hint in case you don't want to go to the trouble of cooking and peeling so many winter squash: Birds Eye makes a frozen package of pureed winter squash that can be used in place of fresh squash. It cuts out a tremendous amount of work.

1 small chopped Vidalia

1 chopped shallot

1 minced clove garlic

2 tablespoons butter

4 cooked, peeled, and pureed butternut squash

6 peeled, cored, and sliced apples

¼ cup sugar

2 cups apple cider

2 cups chicken stock *see index

1 teaspoon pumpkin pie spice

¼ teaspoon nutmeg

2 cups cream

In a soup pot, sauté the onion, shallot, and garlic in the butter. Add the squash, apples, sugar, cider, and stock. Simmer for 30-45 minutes or until the apples are thoroughly cooked. Remove from heat and add spices and cream. Puree in blender carafe until smooth and strain through a sieve.

Serves 12

CREAM OF VIDALIA SOUP

You will never want to see an onion again, but this is well worth all the onion slicing! It is simply delicious! It can be served cold or hot. It has the texture of velvet.

6 cups thinly sliced Vidalias
6 tablespoons butter, divided
1 teaspoon fresh lemon juice
½ cup white wine
1 quart chicken stock *see index
½ teaspoon dried thyme
1 minced clove garlic
½ teaspoon fresh black pepper
1 teaspoon salt
3 tablespoons all-purpose flour
⅔ cup cream

In a soup pot, sauté onions slowly in 3 tablespoons of the butter until tender. Add lemon juice, wine, stock, and seasonings. Simmer 30 minutes. In a small saucepan, make a roux with remaining 3 tablespoons butter and 3 tablespoons flour. Add 1 cup of the soup and stir until blended. Add back to the soup and whisk in. Add cream and simmer until thickened, 20-30 minutes. Puree in blender carafe until smooth and strain through a sieve.

Serves 6

ELEANOR'S CLAM CHOWDER

On a cold winter's day, I don't know if there's anything more satisfying than a big bowl of my mother's chowder with a wedge of hot cornbread.

1 cup chopped Vidalia
4 tablespoons butter, divided
2 tablespoons all-purpose flour
2 cups clam broth
½ cup chopped celery
½ cup grated carrots
1 cup diced and cooked red potatoes
2 cups cream
¼ teaspoon dried thyme
Dash of Tabasco
Dash of Worcestershire
12 ounces fresh diced and steamed clams (if using canned, use the best and drain them)

In a skillet, cook the onions in 2 tablespoons of the butter. Add remaining 2 tablespoons butter and flour to make a roux. Add clam broth and stir until smooth. Add remaining ingredients except clams and simmer until thickened. Add clams just before serving.

Serves 4

WILD RICE AND CHICKEN SOUP

1 chopped Vidalia

1 grated carrot

1 chopped celery stalk

2 tablespoons butter

½ cup all-purpose flour

2 quarts chicken stock *see index

3 cups cooked wild rice**

12 ounces cooked and diced chicken breast

8 ounces sliced fresh button mushrooms

Salt and pepper

In a skillet, sauté vegetables in butter. Add flour and stir until thickened. Add stock and whisk until blended. Add rice, chicken, mushrooms, and season with salt and pepper.

**I also use wild rice broth as part of the stock. I save it when I cook the rice and drain it off. The starch and flavor of the rice help to thicken and season the soup.

Serves 10

ARTICHOKE BISQUE

3 tablespoons chopped Vidalia

8 ounces sliced button mushrooms

3 tablespoons butter

2 tablespoons all-purpose flour

2 cups cream

32 ounces cooked and chopped artichoke hearts, the best

2 cups chicken stock *see index

½ teaspoon dried basil

Salt and pepper

In a skillet, cook onions and mushrooms in butter until just cooked. Add flour to make a roux. Add cream and stir until thickened, 15-20 minutes. In a saucepan, simmer artichokes in chicken stock for 7 minutes. Add to base with seasonings. Puree if you'd rather have a smooth soup.

Serves 6

SPLIT PEA SOUP

Involved and well worth it. A great soup to make on a snowy day! It is the best I've ever had.

Ham stock:
Large ham bone (reserve 2 cups diced ham)
1 bay leaf
1 quartered Vidalia
1 celery stalk
1 peeled carrot
2 whole cloves garlic
Fresh pepper
1 tablespoon chicken base *see Mushroom Gratin
3 pounds dry split peas

In a stock pot, place all ingredients except diced ham and peas. Fill with water. Simmer 2 hours. Strain stock and discard solids. Chill stock, then skim and reserve fat. Reserve 3 quarts of stock, return to soup pot, and bring to a boil. Add peas and cook 45 minutes or until peas are of desired tenderness.

Soup:

1 chopped Vidalia

2 diced carrots

2 chopped celery stalks

1 tablespoon reserved ham fat

1 tablespoon butter

2 minced cloves garlic

Fresh thyme sprigs

Fresh sage sprigs

Dash of cayenne pepper

1 teaspoon celery salt

Salt and pepper

1 quart chicken stock *see index

In a skillet, sauté vegetables in ham fat and butter. Add to ham stock. Add remaining ingredients and simmer 15 minutes. Add reserved ham.

Serves 16

BLACK BEAN SOUP

Super healthy and delicious!

1 cup chopped Vidalia
1 tablespoon olive oil
½ cup chopped celery
½ cup grated carrots
2 cloves minced garlic
16 ounces petite diced tomatoes, including juice
1 cup chicken stock *see index
32 ounces black beans, including liquid
½ teaspoon cumin
Salt and pepper

In a skillet, cook onions in oil. Add celery and carrots and cook until tender. Add remaining ingredients and simmer 25 minutes.

Serves 4

UNITED STATES SENATE BEAN SOUP

In the Senate Dining Room in Washington, D.C., this soup has been a mainstay for over 100 years. It is such a delicious comfort food. I have made it for going on 30 years. If you don't want to make it, a little-known secret is that there's a wonderful canned version available at most grocers — Dominique's U.S. Senate Bean Soup. I enjoy making it from scratch, and there are also usually a few cans of Dominique's in our cabinet in case I want a quick bowl of soup with a grilled cheese.

1½ cups chopped onions

1 clove minced garlic

1 tablespoon butter

1 cup soaked and drained dried navy beans

2 tablespoons chopped fresh parsley

1 sprig fresh thyme

1 bay leaf

¼ cup sliced carrot

2 slices lemon

1 smoked ham hock

Salt and pepper

In a soup pot, sauté the onions and garlic in the butter. Add 1 quart of water and the beans. In a cheesecloth bag, tie up the parsley, thyme, bay leaf, carrot, and lemon. Add the seasoning bag and ham hock to the beans. Bring to a boil and reduce heat to simmer for 3 hours. Remove the bag and ham hock. Season to taste with salt and pepper.

Serves 4

CRÈME FLORENTINE

Men love this soup! It surprised me, but they are often the ones who request this soup the most at the shop. It's very hearty and has lots of flavor!

48 ounces chopped and drained frozen spinach

1 cup chopped Vidalia

1 cup butter

1 cup all-purpose flour

8 cups chicken stock *see index

8 cups half-and-half

Salt and pepper

1 teaspoon Accent

½ teaspoon nutmeg

Pinch of cayenne pepper

In a soup pot, cook onion in butter. Add flour to make a roux. Add stock and half-and-half and stir until smooth. Add seasonings and spinach and simmer 15 minutes to thicken.

Serves 10-12

LOBSTER BISQUE

½ cup minced shallots

3 tablespoons butter

3 tablespoons all-purpose flour

¾ cup white wine

2 cups chicken stock *see index

2 cups clam broth

1 tablespoon cognac

1 bay leaf

½ teaspoon dried thyme

2 tablespoons tomato paste

1½ cups half-and-half

Salt and pepper

1 pound cooked and diced lobster meat

In a soup pot, sauté shallots in butter. Add flour to make a roux. Add wine and reduce. Add chicken stock and clam broth, and whisk to blend. Add cognac, bay leaf, and thyme. Simmer 15 minutes. Add tomato paste and half-and-half, and season with salt and pepper. At the last moment, add lobster meat.

Serves 6

Alternate choices for the lobster:

1) Use shrimp and white corn.

2) Use crab and red bell pepper.

CAMPFIRE CHILI

2½ pounds Angus ground beef

1 chopped large Vidalia

1 chopped red bell pepper

1 chopped yellow bell pepper

2 teaspoons garlic pepper blend

2-4 tablespoons sugar (to taste)

1½ tablespoons chili powder

1½ teaspoons dried basil

2 teaspoons dried oregano

⅛ teaspoon cayenne pepper

1 tablespoon cumin

4 cloves minced garlic

Salt and pepper to taste

32 ounces San Marzano Crushed Tomatoes with puree

1 (14.5-ounce) can Mild Ro*tel Tomatoes and Green Chilies

2 cups beef stock*

15 ounces drained and rinsed black beans

15 ounces drained and rinsed kidney beans

In a soup pot, brown beef. Drain off any fat and return meat to pan. Add onion and sauté until tender. Add remaining vegetables and sauté until tender. Add seasonings, all tomatoes, beef stock, and beans, and simmer for 1-2 hours. Serve with sour cream, grated extra-sharp cheddar, diced red onion, diced avocado, and Tostito strips.

*To make your own beef stock: In a stock pot, place 4 pounds browned beef short ribs, 1 Vidalia, 2 whole carrots, 2 celery stalks, 1 garlic clove, 10 peppercorns, and 1 bay leaf. Fill with water and simmer for 2 hours. Strain stock off and use meat for other purposes.

Makes 2½ quarts

ENTREES

FRIED OYSTERS

CCV, the Country Club of Virginia in Richmond, has the best fried oysters I've ever tasted, hands down. If you get an opportunity, go and eat yourself silly. Otherwise, make some at home with some southern coleslaw and cornbread. You won't be disappointed. You may use this same batter for onion rings or shrimp. I've tried them all with equal success.

12 ounces beer

1½ cups all-purpose flour

Salt and pepper

1 quart fresh shucked oysters

Frying oil

In a medium bowl, mix beer, flour, and seasonings. Let stand at room temperature for 2 hours. Dip oysters in batter and fry until they float. Serve with lemon and tartar sauce.

Serves 4

CAPE CODCAKES

3 pounds cod, poached and broken into pieces

1 medium minced Vidalia

4 minced scallions

2 stalks diced celery

2 diced red bell peppers

½ cup chopped fresh parsley

8 cups fresh bread crumbs, plus additional for coating

3 tablespoons Dijon mustard

1 teaspoon dried thyme

¼ teaspoon cayenne pepper

½ teaspoon Worcestershire

4 eggs

1 cup Duke's mayonnaise

Salt and pepper

In a large bowl, mix all of the ingredients. Form into cakes and lightly coat with the additional bread crumbs. In a skillet, cook codcakes in butter until browned. Serve with lemon slices.

Serves 8-10

CRABCAKES

People rave about my crabcakes. I'm flattered, but guess what? It's not the crabcakes. It's the quality of the crab. Only buy jumbo lump. That's the secret. Don't buy special or backfin; only jumbo lump. Anything you make, use the best ingredients available. That's what makes food taste great, not taking shortcuts.

2 slices Pepperidge Farm White Sandwich Bread
1 pound jumbo lump crab
2 tablespoons Duke's mayonnaise
2 tablespoons finely diced red bell pepper
1 tablespoon finely sliced scallions
1 tablespoon chopped fresh parsley
½ teaspoon Dijon mustard
1 beaten egg
Dash of Worcestershire
Additional bread crumbs for coating
2 tablespoons butter

In a Cuisinart, pulse slices of bread to make fine crumbs. In a medium bowl, lightly toss all of the ingredients except the additional bread crumbs and the butter. Form into 3-ounce cakes and coat with bread crumbs. In a skillet, melt butter and cook crabcakes only until browned on both sides.

Serves 6

CHESAPEAKE CRAB PIE

I lived in Richmond for five years and went to the Chesapeake Bay regularly. You eat a lot of crab when you live in Virginia, which suits me just fine! I ate this once a week or more for a time, I loved it so much!

4 cups cubed Pepperidge Farm White Sandwich Bread

2 tablespoons sherry

1 cup cream

1 pound jumbo lump crab

½ cup melted butter

Grated rind and juice of 1 lemon

Salt and pepper

Half-and-half

In a bowl, sprinkle bread with sherry. Add cream and soak for 30 minutes. In a buttered gratin or other shallow baking dish, alternate layers of bread, crab, butter, lemon rind and juice, salt, and pepper. Repeat, ending with a layer of bread. Fill dish with half-and-half to within ½-inch of the top. Bake 40-60 minutes until puffed and golden.

Serves 6

CORN CREPES WITH SHRIMP AND GREEN CHILIES

From the kitchen of Gretchen Langslet. Gretch, my favorite walking buddy, made these one night, and we all loved them. I've made them with chicken and made the filling with flour tortillas in a hurry. They're great no matter how you make them!

Crepes:

1¼ cups whole milk

¾ cup yellow cornmeal

2 eggs

⅓ cup all-purpose flour

1 teaspoon sugar

¼ teaspoon salt

4 tablespoons melted butter, divided

In a blender carafe, blend first six ingredients with 2 tablespoons of the butter until smooth. Let mixture stand 20 minutes. Heat 6-inch crepe pan and brush with part of the remaining butter. Spoon 3 tablespoons of batter into the pan and cook until browned on both sides. Repeat until all of the batter is used.

Sauce:

2 tablespoons butter

2 (4-ounce) cans diced green chilies

½ cup minced scallions

1 clove minced garlic

2 tablespoons all-purpose flour

1 cup chicken stock *see index

1 cup cream

1 cup sour cream

Salt and pepper to taste

1½ pounds peeled, deveined, steamed shrimp

9 ounces grated sharp cheddar cheese

In a large saucepan, melt butter and sauté chilies, scallions, and garlic 5 minutes. Add flour and stir for 3 minutes. Mix in stock and bring to a boil. Reduce heat and simmer until sauce is smooth. Add cream and simmer until thick. Add sour cream, salt, and pepper; remove from heat. Stir in shrimp and 1 cup cheddar. Fill each crepe with 3 tablespoons shrimp mix. Place in a greased 9-by-13-inch pan, top with remaining sauce, and sprinkle with remaining cheddar. Bake at 350 degrees for 15-20 minutes.

Serves 6

JEKYLL ISLAND SHRIMP

As a child, I spent time every summer at Jekyll Island. It was an oasis, undiscovered and peaceful, with plenty of golf nearby for my parents as my brother and I spent all day on the beach collecting shells and making friends. We went to the same fabulous restaurant most nights. I ordered this shrimp over and over, and to this day, if asked what my last supper would be, this is it. As I grew older and we lived in Chapel Hill, I discovered that the old Danziger restaurant the Villa Teo made a very similar shrimp to that of my childhood memories. Again, it's the only thing I ever ordered at the Villa Teo. It is my very favorite of all!

½ cup softened butter

1 clove minced garlic

⅔ cup bread crumbs

2 tablespoons chopped fresh parsley

⅓ cup sherry

Dash of cayenne pepper

2 pounds peeled, deveined, and cooked shrimp

In a bowl, mix all of the ingredients except the shrimp. Place the shrimp in the bottom of a 9-by-13-inch Pyrex. Spread the butter mixture over the shrimp evenly. Bake at 350 degrees for 20-25 minutes or until the topping is golden.

Serves 6

PAELLA

2 cups white wine

6 raw clams in the shell

6 raw mussels in the shell

½ pound raw shrimp in the shell

2 pounds chicken wings, tips removed

Olive oil

1 chopped Vidalia

2 peeled and diced tomatoes

½ pound diced pancetta

Salt and pepper

1½ cups arborio rice (risotto – short grain)

½ cup blanched fresh green beans

3½ cups chicken stock *see index

Pinch of saffron threads

In a covered saucepan, bring white wine to a boil. Add clams and steam only until clams open. Remove clams immediately. In the same wine, steam mussels only until mussels open. Remove immediately. Reserve wine. Set aside shellfish for later use. In a skillet, cook chicken in 2 tablespoons olive oil until browned. Set chicken aside. In same skillet in 1 tablespoon olive oil, cook onion until tender.

Add tomatoes, pancetta, salt, and pepper. Add chicken to tomato mixture and simmer 10 minutes. In skillet, cook arborio rice in 1 tablespoon olive oil until lightly browned. Stir constantly. In a paella pan, layer the rice, the tomato/chicken mix, and the green beans. Top with chicken stock. Add wine from shellfish and the saffron. Cover and bake at 350 degrees for 15 minutes. Remove from oven and arrange raw shrimp over the top. Cover and return to oven for 15 minutes or until the shrimp are just cooked through. Remove from oven and arrange clams and mussels across the top. All liquid should have been absorbed. If it needs extra cooking, return to oven until arborio is al dente and all liquid has been absorbed.

Serves 6

MAINE LOBSTER SALAD

Any chance I get, I head to Maine. I just adore it. One of my favorite things is getting fresh lobster rolls at roadside stands. The clam shacks really have some of the best food. This is the true and simple lobster salad they pile in a hoagie roll. What makes it so delicious is the addition of a little melted butter. The reason it's simple and not heavily spiced? Because fresh lobster doesn't need a thing. You want to be able to taste its sweetness. Don't doctor this up. Buy fresh lobster and cook it about 8 minutes. Do not cook it 15; it's entirely too long, and too many people overcook lobster. Spoon the salad over Boston or Bibb lettuce if you don't want the bread. Close your eyes and just savor the lobster. My dear friend Candace got married in Maine, and we couldn't get enough lobster rolls. We even had North Carolina BBQ and Maine lobster rolls for her rehearsal dinner. The best of both worlds!

1 pound cooked and diced lobster meat

¼ cup celery

¼ cup Duke's mayonnaise

2 teaspoons fresh lemon juice

Salt and pepper

2 teaspoons melted butter

In a medium bowl, mix all together and serve immediately on soft hoagie rolls or over lettuce.

Serves 4

CHICKEN CURRY

*As unlikely as it may seem, I have made this since I was a little girl. Curry is a distinctive flavor and not everyone loves it, but served over rice with lots of toppings, it makes for a fun and delicious dinner party. Diced cucumbers, golden raisins, currants, toasted almonds, chutney, large coconut flakes . . .
the sky is the limit! People adore parties that are participatory. Enjoy!*

1 cup chopped Vidalia

1 cup chopped celery

½ chopped green pepper

3 tablespoons butter

3 tablespoons flour

1 peeled and finely chopped apple

2 tablespoons lemon juice

1 quart chicken stock *see index

1-pound can petite diced tomatoes with juice

3 cups diced cooked chicken breast

1 cup tiny green peas

2 tablespoons curry powder

In a skillet, cook onions, celery, and green pepper in butter. Add the flour and cook until it forms a roux, even though the vegetables are in the pan. Add the apple, lemon juice, and the stock. Stir until blended and thickened. Add the tomatoes and curry powder and simmer 15 minutes. Add the chicken and peas last, cooking until heated through. Serve with rice.

Serves 6

Take to Friends

GREEK CHICKEN

From the kitchen of Betsy Bowman. I was in the middle of moving and came home one night, after unpacking at the new house, to the previous house, where I was still staying. There was a cooler at my garage door with dinner in it. I can't tell you what else was in the cooler; I didn't eat it or even look at it. When I opened the cooler and smelled the Greek chicken, I ate it standing over the cooler with my fingers and polished off every morsel on the bones. It is simply the most wonderful chicken I have ever had, from the most wonderful friend I have ever had. If you want to do your friends a favor, take them dinner when they're moving. They'll remember it forever.

4 chicken breasts on the bone

8-10 garlic cloves, sliced

2-3 lemons, 2 juiced and 1 sliced

1 tablespoon oregano

½ cup olive oil

Place chicken breasts and remaining ingredients in a 10-by-14-inch baking dish. Bake at 350 degrees for 1½ hours, basting occasionally. Chicken should be browned and crispy.

Serves 4

RASPBERRY CHICKEN

2 tablespoons butter
2 flattened boneless chicken breasts
¼ cup chopped Vidalia
4 tablespoons raspberry vinegar, the best
¼ cup chicken stock*
¼ cup heavy cream
1 tablespoon San Marzano Crushed Tomatoes
½ cup fresh raspberries
Mint leaves

In a skillet, melt the butter and cook the chicken breasts for 3-5 minutes or until golden. Add the onion, lower the heat, and continue cooking for 15 minutes. Add the vinegar, raise the heat to medium, and deglaze the pan until the vinegar has reduced to about 2 tablespoons. Whisk in chicken stock, cream, and tomatoes, and simmer for 1 minute until the sauce has blended thoroughly. Serve chicken garnished with fresh raspberries, mint leaves and sauce drizzled over the top.

*To make your own chicken stock, place a whole chicken, 1 Vidalia, 2 whole carrots, 2 celery stalks, 1 garlic clove, 10 peppercorns, and 1 bay leaf in a stock pot. Fill with water and simmer for 2 hours. Strain stock off and use meat for other purposes.

Serves 2

EAST GRACE STREET CHICKEN WITH SPINACH FETTUCCINI

4 boneless chicken breasts

Butter

1 small chopped Vidalia

½ cup sliced button mushrooms

½ cup chopped green bell pepper

½ cup white wine

2 teaspoons Dijon mustard

½ teaspoon paprika

¼ teaspoon dry mustard

Dash of Tabasco

Salt and pepper

1 cup sour cream

1 pound cooked spinach fettuccini

In a skillet, sauté chicken breasts in butter until thoroughly cooked, about 15 minutes. Remove from pan. Add vegetables and cook until tender. Add wine and reduce. Add seasonings and sour cream and stir to blend. Slice chicken and return to the pan. Add fettuccini and toss all together.

Serves 4

PORK L'ORANGE

4 boneless pork chops, each 1-inch thick
Salt and pepper
Paprika
2 tablespoons canola oil
⅓ cup water
½ cup sugar
½ teaspoon cornstarch
½ teaspoon cinnamon
4 teaspoons grated orange rind
1 cup orange juice
1 teaspoon whole cloves

Sprinkle chops with salt, pepper, and paprika. In a skillet, heat oil and brown chops. Add water, cover, and simmer 30 minutes. In a saucepan, mix remaining ingredients and bring to a boil until thickened. Spoon over chops and serve with rice.

Serves 4

RIBS

These are not at all like grilled ribs. The meat falls off the bones and is so tender you won't believe it. I keep thinking I'll try and grill the ribs with the seasoning, but the best part about these is the pan juices. Perhaps wrapping the vegetables in foil and doing them on the grill and doing the ribs with the seasoning would work, but I just can't get past how great they taste like this to try anything different. I've made them this way for so many years. At about five hours, I start to peek and taste. The house will smell so incredible you won't be able to help yourself diving into the pan. The jalapenos and garlic become somewhat sweet after cooking for so long. I usually make some homemade BBQ sauce to eat with the ribs but, truthfully, the pan juices are so wonderful you don't need it. This does require some planning due to the marinating time and the long cook time. I try and get them in the oven late morning . . . it's the waiting part that's so difficult.

2 teaspoons Spike Gourmet Natural Seasoning

1 teaspoon Accent

½ teaspoon pepper

5 pounds baby back pork ribs

2 sliced large Vidalias

6 cloves minced garlic

2 minced jalapeno peppers

2 sliced green bell peppers

2 sliced red bell peppers

2 sliced yellow bell peppers

In a small bowl, mix the seasonings. Line a large roasting pan with enough foil to wrap completely around all the ribs. Spread a layer of onions, garlic, and peppers on top of the foil. Sprinkle with a little bit of the seasoning mix. Place a layer of ribs on the vegetables. Continue to layer the onions, garlic, peppers, seasoning, and ribs. Sprinkle the top of the last layer with more seasoning. Tightly wrap the marinated ribs in the foil and refrigerate for 6 hours. Remove the pan from the refrigerator and let it sit at room temperature for 30 minutes. Preheat the oven to 400 degrees. Just before placing the ribs in the oven, reduce the temperature to 300 degrees. Bake the foil-wrapped ribs for 6-8 hours. Serve with the vegetables and pan juices and your favorite BBQ sauce if desired.

Serves 8-10

OSSO BUCO

Traditional Osso Buco is made with veal shanks. I prefer to use lean veal stew meat. There is no bone and no fat. Your butcher will be happy to cut some lean meat for you into small cubes.

Salt and pepper
Flour for dusting veal
5 pounds cubed veal stew meat
Olive oil
1½ cups chopped Vidalia
½ cup chopped carrots
½ cup chopped celery
4 tablespoons butter
2 cloves minced garlic
1 cup white wine
¾ cup chicken stock *see index
½ teaspoon dried thyme
3 cups diced petite tomatoes, including juice
2 bay leaves

Gremolata:

1 tablespoon grated lemon rind

1 clove minced garlic

3 tablespoons chopped fresh parsley

In a dutch oven, sauté seasoned, floured veal in olive oil until browned. Set aside. In same pan, sauté vegetables in butter until tender. Mix all ingredients in the pot and put a lid on it. Bake at 350 degrees for 1¼ hours. In a bowl, mix gremolata ingredients and serve a spoonful on each portion.

Serves 10

SOUTHERN DINER MEATLOAF

1 large chopped Vidalia

1 chopped red bell pepper

5 minced garlic cloves

3 tablespoons olive oil

3 pounds ground angus beef

3 beaten eggs

⅓ cup cream

2½ tablespoons soy sauce

1½ teaspoons salt

1 teaspoon pepper

1½ cups fresh bread crumbs

Topping:

½ cup tomato paste

½ cup crushed tomatoes

Salt and pepper

In a skillet, sauté onion, red bell pepper, and garlic in oil until tender. Let cool. In a large bowl, mix beef, eggs, cream, seasonings, and bread crumbs. Add cooled vegetables. Shape into meatloaf pan. Bake at 325 degrees for 1½ hours. In a bowl, mix topping ingredients. Add topping and bake for 10 minutes.

Serves 8

BEEF BOURGUIGNON

Once upon a time, a friend was at my house for dinner and I had made Beef Bourguignon. She said, "What's in it?" Not thinking she was asking for the recipe but just a general description, I said, "Filet and red wine." She went home and threw some filet and red wine in a pot and called to tell me her husband was not impressed, nor did it taste like mine. I wasn't trying to keep the recipe from her, but didn't know she was asking exactly how to make it. It is a lot of trouble but truly one of the great pleasures in life. Rich to beat the band, but comfort food in grand style.

2½ pounds filet mignon, cut in 1-inch dice, salted and peppered

Olive oil

2 medium chopped Vidalias

2 tablespoons butter

2 cloves minced garlic

2 cups beef stock *see index

3 cups burgundy, the best

½ cup cognac, the best

2 tablespoons tomato paste

1 teaspoon dried thyme

Salt and pepper to taste

To finish:

4 tablespoons butter, divided

3 tablespoons all-purpose flour

12 ounces button mushrooms, cleaned and sliced

In a dutch oven, sauté the beef in olive oil in small batches until browned. Set aside. Add the onions and sauté in butter until lightly browned. In the dutch oven, put the beef, onions, garlic, beef stock, wine, cognac, tomato paste, and thyme. Cover and bake at 325 degrees for 3 hours. Taste to be sure the meat is tender. Bake longer if needed. To finish: In a small saucepan, make a roux with 3 tablespoons of the butter and the flour. Add to the beef and blend in. Return to oven for 30 minutes to thicken the pan juices. In a sauté pan, sauté the mushrooms in the remaining 1 tablespoon butter until barely cooked. Add to the beef and season with salt and pepper. Serve over rice.

Serves 6

BEEF KABOBS

Marinade:

¼ cup salad oil

2 tablespoons red wine vinegar

1 teaspoon onion salt

1 teaspoon celery salt

¼ teaspoon pepper

¾ teaspoon garlic salt

1 tablespoon soy sauce

Kabobs:

1 pound cubed filet mignon

1 thickly sliced zucchini

1 cubed green bell pepper

1 cubed red bell pepper

1 cubed medium Vidalia

In a bowl, mix the marinade ingredients. Place all the kabob ingredients in a large freezer Ziploc and pour in the marinade. Seal tightly and refrigerate for 4 hours. Drain the tidbits and alternate them on metal skewers. Grill according to your taste preference.

Serves 4

SPAGHETTI SAUCE

2 pounds ground Angus beef

2 diced Vidalias

1 chopped green bell pepper

1 chopped red bell pepper

2 chopped stalks celery

3 cloves minced garlic

1 teaspoon salt

1 teaspoon fresh black pepper

1 bay leaf

1 teaspoon dried thyme

1 teaspoon dried parsley

½ teaspoon dried sage

1 teaspoon Worcestershire

1-2 teaspoons sugar

½ teaspoon celery salt

Pinch of cayenne pepper

2 (28-ounce) cans lightly pureed San Marzano Whole Peeled Tomatoes

2 (6-ounce) cans tomato paste

2 (6-ounce) cans warm water

In a large dutch oven, brown beef. Drain off any fat and return meat to pan. Add onion and sauté until tender. Add remaining vegetables and sauté until tender. Add seasonings, tomatoes, tomato paste, and water. Simmer for 1-2 hours. Serve with pasta and parmesan.

Serves 10

CREAMY TOMATO SAUCE

1 small chopped Vidalia
2 tablespoons olive oil
1 clove minced garlic
14 ounces chef-style tomatoes
1 tablespoon sliced fresh basil
1 teaspoon sugar
½ teaspoon dried oregano
½ teaspoon salt
¼ teaspoon fresh ground pepper
½ cup heavy cream
½ pound cooked fettuccini
Freshly shredded parmesan

In a skillet, cook the onion in olive oil. Add garlic and cook for 1 minute. Add remaining ingredients except for fettuccini and parmesan. Simmer but do not boil. Serve over pasta with lots of parmesan.

Serves 4-6

MARINARA

½ chopped Vidalia

1 clove minced garlic

2 tablespoons olive oil

1 grated carrot

2 tablespoons chopped green pepper

1 bay leaf

1 teaspoon dried oregano

½ teaspoon dried thyme

½ teaspoon dried basil

2 tablespoons chopped fresh parsley

2 cups chopped tomatoes

6 ounces tomato paste

Salt and pepper

1 teaspoon sugar

In a dutch oven, cook onion and garlic in oil. Add remaining ingredients and simmer for 30 minutes. Serve with pasta and parmesan.

Serves 8

EGGPLANT PARMESAN

I have made Eggplant Parmesan for years by this method. I love to try it everywhere, but I like mine because there is no breading. It's lighter and healthier! I also have been known to oil a cookie sheet and cook the eggplant in the oven. You can cook it all at once, which saves time.

Salt

2 pounds sliced eggplant

Olive oil

2 cups ricotta

2 eggs

½ cup shredded parmesan

¼ cup chopped fresh parsley

Marinara *see index

½ pound shredded mozzarella

Pepper

Salt the eggplant slices and place in a colander to drain for 30 minutes. There are bitter enzymes that will be released and improve the flavor of your eggplant. Rinse thoroughly and towel dry. In a skillet, heat oil and sauté eggplant until tender. In a medium bowl, mix ricotta, eggs, parmesan, pepper, and parsley.

In a 9-by-13-inch Pyrex, layer marinara, eggplant, ricotta mix, and mozzarella, ending with marinara and mozzarella. Bake at 350 degrees for 30-40 minutes until brown and bubbly.

Serves 6

ON THE SIDE

BLACK BEAN CAKES

1 small chopped onion

1 chopped red bell pepper

4 minced garlic cloves

Olive oil

1 teaspoon cumin

Dash of Tabasco

Salt and pepper

1½ cups cooked and drained black beans

1 cup cooked rice

In a skillet, sauté onion, red pepper, and garlic in olive oil until tender. Add seasonings. In a Cuisinart, pulse beans until coarsely chopped. Add rice and cooked vegetables and pulse until blended. Form bean mixture into cakes. In the skillet, sauté cakes in olive oil until lightly browned on both sides and heated throughout. Serve with salsa, grated cheddar, and sour cream. You may also want to treat these as burgers on a bun with cheese and the usual condiments.

Serves 4

PINEAPPLE BAKED BEANS

1 medium chopped Vidalia

1 chopped green pepper

8 slices cooked bacon, broken into pieces, grease reserved

32 ounces Bush's Original Baked Beans

16 ounces drained and rinsed black beans

16 ounces drained and rinsed kidney beans

20 ounces drained, crushed pineapple

1 peeled, cored, and diced apple

½ cup mild chunky salsa

1 tablespoon Dijon mustard

½ cup brown sugar

In a skillet, cook onions and peppers in 1 tablespoon bacon grease. Mix all ingredients and put in a 10-by-14-inch Pyrex. Bake at 350 degrees for 45 minutes or until bubbly around the edges.

Serves 10-12

SALAD BURRITOS

The first time I had these, we were on a boat water skiing, and they were the perfect picnic food. They are so delicious, so light and healthy. The bean mixture alone is also a great summer salad. Some people I've made them for heat them before adding the lettuce.

Filling:

16-ounce can drained and rinsed black beans

16-ounce can drained and rinsed kidney beans

16-ounce can drained and rinsed chickpeas

½ medium chopped Vidalia

½ chopped green bell pepper

½ chopped red bell pepper

1 cup canola oil

6 tablespoons cider vinegar

1 package taco seasoning

1 tablespoon sugar or to taste

In a large bowl, mix all ingredients. Chill for 2 hours.

To assemble:

Flavored wraps (spinach, tomato, jalapeno)

4 cups shredded lettuce

8 ounces shredded Mexican cheese blend

Drain beans and spoon into wraps. Add lettuce and cheese, then roll up.

Serves 6-8

STUFFED ACORN SQUASH

1 chopped medium Vidalia

½ cup chopped celery

2 tablespoons butter

2 peeled, cored, and diced Braeburn apples

½ cup dried cranberries

½ cup brown sugar

2 teaspoons cinnamon

1 teaspoon ginger

½ cup chopped walnuts

4 halves cooked and seeded acorn squash

In a skillet, cook onion and celery in butter. Add remaining ingredients except for squash halves. Fill squash. Place squash on a cookie sheet. Bake at 350 degrees for 40 minutes.

Serves 4

BOURBON SWEET POTATOES

5 peeled, parboiled, and sliced sweet potatoes

¾ cup sugar

¾ cup brown sugar

½ cup butter

2-3 tablespoons bourbon

2-3 tablespoons water

Place sweet potatoes in a greased 8-inch-square pan. In a saucepan, boil remaining ingredients until sugars melt. Pour sauce over sweet potatoes and bake at 350 degrees until well glazed, 45 minutes or more. You may also puree them once baked.

Serves 6-8

PARTY POTATOES

These are the best mashed potatoes ever. Healthy? No. Delicious? Yes. I have even made them into the shape of a birthday cake complete with candles for a friend's son who adores them! The ultimate comfort food with meatloaf, roasted chicken, or grilled filet mignon.

5 pounds peeled and cooked Yukon gold potatoes
8 ounces cream cheese
2 ounces sour cream
5 tablespoons chopped chives
2 tablespoons butter
Salt and pepper

In a stand mixer, blend all of the ingredients until smooth. Season with salt and pepper. Spoon into an 8-inch-square buttered dish and bake at 350 degrees for 20-30 minutes.

Serves 10

CAULIFLOWER GRATIN

1 tablespoon white wine vinegar

Head of cauliflower broken into florets

5 tablespoons melted butter

Salt and pepper

1 cup sour cream

1 cup buttered fresh bread crumbs

In a dutch oven filled with boiling water and the vinegar, cook cauliflower until just tender. Drain thoroughly. Mix florets with butter, plenty of salt and pepper, and sour cream. Spoon into an 8-inch-square dish and sprinkle with bread crumbs. Bake at 350 degrees for 20-30 minutes or until browned.

Serves 6

GINGERED CARROTS

1 pound peeled baby carrots

¼ cup melted butter

3 pieces minced crystallized ginger

⅓ cup brown sugar

In a saucepan, boil carrots until just tender. Drain, return to pan with remaining ingredients, and toss to coat.

Serves 4-6

STUFFED ZUCCHINI

In my garden, I purposefully leave some zucchini to grow oversized. They're perfect for stuffing if they grow to be about three inches in diameter. This is a treat! Be sure and use your homegrown tomatoes and basil, too!

2 overgrown zucchini sliced into 2-inch rounds
Salt and pepper
Olive oil or butter
1 medium chopped Vidalia
5 cloves minced garlic
3 cored, seeded, and chopped tomatoes
⅓ cup chopped fresh basil leaves
2 cups grated Monterey Jack cheese
Parmesan

Season the zucchini with salt and pepper. In a skillet, cook zucchini in oil 2 minutes on each side and set aside. In same pan, cook onion until tender. Add remaining ingredients off heat and toss. Using a large spoon, remove some flesh from the center of each slice of zucchini. Fill each slice with tomato mixture. Sprinkle with parmesan. Place on greased cookie sheet and bake at 350 degrees for 15-20 minutes.

Serves 4-6

RATATOUILLE

I have the advantage of having a large garden for the shop where I can pick almost all of these ingredients fresh the morning I make the ratatouille. If you don't have your own garden, buy the ingredients at your local farmers' market. It will make all the difference in the world.

Salt

4 small cubed eggplant

2 medium chopped Vidalias

7 medium cubed zucchini

2 cubed red bell peppers

2 cubed green bell peppers

Olive oil

2 tablespoons minced fresh garlic

3 pounds peeled plum tomatoes

6 ounces tomato paste

¼ cup chopped parsley

2 tablespoons dried basil

2 tablespoons dried oregano

Pepper

Salt the eggplant cubes and place in a colander to drain for 30 minutes. There are bitter enzymes that will be released and improve the flavor of your eggplant. Rinse thoroughly and towel dry. In a large bowl, mix all vegetables except tomatoes and sprinkle with olive oil until all pieces are slightly oiled. On a large jellyroll pan, spread out vegetables and bake at 375 until just tender, 30 minutes or so. Transfer to a large soup pot and add remaining ingredients. Simmer 10-20 minutes until all of the flavors meld. The flavor will improve the longer all the mix is together. Serve hot or room temperature.

Serves 8-10

BAKED TOMATOES

8 vine-ripe tomato halves

2 tablespoons melted butter

2 teaspoons sugar

½ teaspoon salt

½ teaspoon fresh ground pepper

2 tablespoons chopped fresh parsley

2 cloves minced garlic

2 tablespoons vinegar

Fresh bread crumbs to top

Place tomatoes cut side up on cookie sheet. Mix remaining ingredients except bread crumbs and spoon over the top of each tomato. Sprinkle with bread crumbs and bake at 375 degrees for 15-20 minutes or until bread crumbs are browned.

Serves 8

ROASTED ASPARAGUS

1 pound trimmed and washed asparagus*

Olive oil

Sea salt

Fresh ground pepper

On a jellyroll pan, place the asparagus in a single layer. Sprinkle with oil and lightly salt and pepper. Bake at 400 degrees for 7 minutes. Bake longer if you don't like your asparagus a little al dente. Serve hot or room temperature. Leave the stalks in a single layer or they will continue to cook if you stack them.

Serves 6

Optional drizzles after cooking:

1) Drizzle with aged balsamic vinegar.
2) Drizzle with freshly squeezed orange juice.

*The traditional method of trimming asparagus is to hold the stalk near the base and bend until it snaps. It will break off exactly at the point where the tough bottom meets the tender stalk. It may not please you as the stalks may not be all one length using this method, but it ensures the asparagus will all be edible and tender, not leaving a pile of tough ends on your plate. You may also use a vegetable peeler to trim the bottom one-third of the stalk of the nubs. If using pencil-thin stalks, no trimming is necessary, and the roasting time could be as low as 5 minutes.

BROCCOLI TAGLIERINI

2 cloves minced garlic

½ cup butter

1 pound steamed broccoli florets

8 ounces cooked fettuccini

1 cup shredded fresh parmesan

In a skillet, cook garlic in butter. Add remaining ingredients and toss thoroughly.

Serves 6

ORIENTAL PASTA SALAD

Dressing:

⅓ cup vegetable oil

⅓ cup soy sauce

2 tablespoons sugar, or more to taste

1 teaspoon sesame oil

¼ teaspoon red pepper flakes

¼ cup grated fresh ginger*

2 teaspoons minced garlic

Salad:

1 pound cooked and drained fettuccini

¼ pound blanched snow peas (30 seconds in boiling water)

1 julienned red bell pepper

1 (8-ounce) can drained diced water chestnuts

½ cup sliced scallions

2 cups bite-sized broccoli florets

2 teaspoons toasted sesame seeds

Optional:

Grilled chicken, beef or shrimp

In a Cuisinart, mix all dressing ingredients. (I add more sugar.) Mix salad ingredients in a bowl and add dressing. Chill 2 hours before serving.

*The easiest way to grate fresh ginger is to peel the ginger with a vegetable peeler and cut it into pieces. Place the pieces in a Cuisinart and pulse until finely grated.

Serves 6

TABOULI

1 cup uncooked bulgur

½ cup olive oil

½ cup fresh lemon juice

1 cup chopped scallions

1 cup diced celery

1 cup chopped fresh parsley

1 cup chopped fresh mint leaves

3 diced tomatoes

3 diced green bell peppers

2 diced cucumbers

1 teaspoon fresh black pepper

2 teaspoons salt

The only way this recipe works is if you layer the ingredients in the order in which they're listed, beginning with the bulgur. Layer in a straight-sided bowl, then cover and refrigerate for 24 hours. Stir thoroughly and serve cold.

Serves 8-10

SOUTHERN COLESLAW

1 pound finely shredded savoy cabbage

1 cup finely shredded red cabbage

1 cup finely shredded carrots

2 tablespoons grated Vidalia

⅓ cup sugar

½ teaspoon salt

⅛ teaspoon fresh pepper

¼ cup whole milk

½ cup Duke's mayonnaise

1½ tablespoons cider vinegar

2½ tablespoons fresh lemon juice

In a large bowl, mix all of the ingredients. Chill until ready to serve.

Serves 8

Optional additions:

1) Blue cheese and pecans
2) Raisins and mandarin oranges
3) Dill pickles and minced garlic
4) Feta, diced cucumbers, and tomatoes

GRAPEFRUIT SALAD

From the kitchen of Susan Aldridge, one of my best friends and my favorite house to be invited to for dinner! We always have this at my house for Thanksgiving. It is so refreshing and a nice addition to the heavier things we have on Turkey Day! I eat it all by itself in the summer; it's a meal for me on a hot day!

1 cup boiling water

1 cup sugar

4 packages unflavored gelatin, softened in 1 cup cold water

6 grapefruit, peeled and sectioned, all pith removed

1 cup chopped pecans

20-ounce can crushed pineapple (do not drain)

Mix boiling water and sugar. Pour over softened gelatin. In a large bowl mix all of the ingredients. Pour into 9-by-13-inch dish and chill until firm.

Serves 8-10

CORNUCOPIA SALAD

From the kitchen of Barbara Hardin. I have had the tremendous blessing over the years of becoming friends with many of my clients. Paul and Barbara Hardin moved to Chapel Hill for Paul to become the chancellor of UNC, and we've been dear friends ever since. Barbara is a fabulous cook and a terrific hostess, and I've enjoyed this salad at her house. I called her and begged to include it so you can enjoy it as much as I have!

½ head Boston or Bibb lettuce

½ head romaine lettuce

1 cup chopped celery

4 chopped scallions

11 ounces drained and chilled mandarin oranges

1 diced avocado

1 cored, peeled, and diced apple

½ cup crumbled Danish blue cheese

3 cooked and diced boneless chicken breasts

On individual salad plates, arrange the ingredients evenly divided. Top with almonds and dressing.

Candied Almonds:

3 tablespoons sugar

½ cup sliced almonds

In a skillet, melt sugar with almonds, stirring constantly until almonds are coated. Be careful not to burn the sugar. Remove from heat and spread in single layer on racks to cool.

Dressing:

¼ cup canola oil

2 tablespoons white wine vinegar

1 tablespoon chopped fresh parsley

½ teaspoon salt

½ teaspoon pepper

In a bowl, whisk all of the ingredients together.

Serves 4

CRANBERRY LIME SAUCE

1 pound washed fresh cranberries

2 cups sugar

1 teaspoon lime zest

1 teaspoon orange zest

¼ cup fresh lime juice

¼ cup fresh orange juice

½ cup water

In a large saucepan, combine all of the ingredients and bring to a boil. Reduce heat and simmer until all of the berries have popped. Cool and store. Serve chilled.

Serves 12

CINNAMON APPLE SALAD

1 3-ounce package strawberry Jell-O

½ cup Cinnamon Imperials

2 cups boiling water

1½ cups diced Braeburn apples

1 cup diced celery

½ cups chopped pecans

Dissolve Jell-O and candy in boiling water. Chill. When the mixture begins to gel, add apples, celery, and nuts. Chill until firm.

Serves 8

SWEET TOOTH

BOURBON PRALINES

I think anything involving using a candy thermometer requires great patience and the perfect dry day. Humidity can ruin any boiled sugar mixture. These make a terrific Christmas present!

2 cups sugar

1 teaspoon baking soda

1 cup buttermilk

Pinch of salt

2 tablespoons butter

2½ cups pecans

5 tablespoons bourbon

In a saucepan, combine sugar, soda, buttermilk, and salt. Cook with a candy thermometer to 210 degrees. Add butter and pecans and continue to cook, stirring constantly, to 230 degrees. Remove from heat and stir in bourbon. Cool about 1 minute. Beat by hand until mixture thickens, about 5 minutes. Drop by tablespoons on greased cookie sheets. Let stand until firm.

Serves 12-14

WHITE CHOCOLATE BREAD PUDDING

4 cups whole milk

2 cups cream

6 whole eggs

4 egg yolks

1 cup sugar

1 teaspoon salt

1 teaspoon vanilla

1 loaf challah bread

24 ounces white chocolate pieces

In a saucepan, steep milk and cream. Gradually add in eggs and yolks. Add sugar, salt, and vanilla. In a greased 9-by-13-inch pan, add bread cubes and sprinkle with chocolate pieces. Pour milk mix over bread and let soak for 30 minutes. Bake at 350 degrees for 30-45 minutes or until set.

Serves 8-10

*Optional: dried cranberries and toasted almonds blended in with bread cubes

BANANA PUDDING

This is my favorite banana pudding recipe, though I have many. The custard is light and fluffy. I often serve it at parties at my home in giant wine goblets. You can dust with shaved chocolate over the whipped cream to gild the lily!

2 cups whole milk

½ vanilla bean

6 egg yolks (save whites, if desired, to make a meringue)

1 cup plus 2 tablespoons sugar, divided

¼ cup cornstarch

1 tablespoon butter

Nilla Vanilla Wafers

2 sliced bananas

1 cup cream

2 tablespoons sugar

In a saucepan, combine milk and vanilla bean and bring to a simmer. Remove from heat and let sit 30 minutes for vanilla bean to flavor the milk. Remove the vanilla bean. In a large bowl, whisk the egg yolks and 1 cup sugar together until light and fluffy. Add the cornstarch. Temper with ¼ cup hot milk. Whisk all of the remaining hot milk into the yolks. Mix thoroughly. Return milk mixture to the saucepan and bring to a boil slowly. It will thicken all of a sudden just when you think it will *never* thicken. Remove from heat, add butter, and whisk to blend. Pour through a nylon sieve to remove any lumps. Layer wafers, bananas, and custard. Top with cream that has been whipped and sweetened with 2 tablespoons sugar or use egg whites to make a meringue.

Serves 8

BANANAS FOSTER

4 tablespoons butter

3 tablespoons brown sugar

4 sliced bananas

2 tablespoons banana liqueur

Dash of cinnamon

3 tablespoons dark rum

Vanilla ice cream, the best

In a skillet, heat butter and brown sugar until sugar is melted. Add bananas and cook until heated through. Add banana liqueur and cinnamon and swirl. Add rum; don't stir. Dipping a stainless spoon into the pan, light a match to only the alcohol on the spoon, and light the pan of alcohol with the lit spoon. Shake gently until the flames cover the entire surface of the pan and swirl until the flames go out. Spoon bananas and pan sauce over the vanilla ice cream in individual dishes.

Serves 6

FLAMED STRAWBERRIES

2 tablespoons honey

2 tablespoons butter

1 tablespoon Grand Marnier

1 teaspoon grated orange rind

1 tablespoon water

1 tablespoon brandy

3 cups sliced strawberries

Mint leaves

In a saucepan, mix honey, butter, Grand Marnier, orange rind, and water. Bring to a boil for 30 seconds. Add brandy and light. Shake until the flames die down and the sauce has thickened. Serve strawberries in stemmed glassware with sauce and mint leaves.

Serves 8

LEMON ICEBOX PIE

This may seem rather fifties, but my mother made it often when we were young, and I find I can't keep it in the shop in the summer. It's light and citrusy and just the right amount of dessert to satisfy any sweet tooth. You may also spoon the filling into giant stemmed goblets and top with berries and mint leaves for another version.

2 separated eggs

½ cup sugar

¼ cup lemon juice

1 cup cream, whipped

Graham crust (better yet, a crust made with Lemon Cooler cookies)

In a large bowl, mix yolks, sugar, and juice. Fold in whipped cream. In a separate bowl, beat whites until stiff and fold into mixture. Turn into graham crust and freeze. Serve frozen.

Serves 6

PEANUT BUTTER PIE

In the shop people always think this is a kids' dessert. Then they buy it once, and they're hooked. Though kids may love it, I would go so far as to say it's one of my favorite desserts. To gild the lily, serve with tons of whipped cream and hot fudge — even broken Reese's cups if you dare.

2 cups confectioners' sugar

8 ounces cream cheese

1 cup whole milk

1 cup peanut butter

1 cup cream, whipped and sweetened

Oreo crust

To top:

Chocolate syrup

½ **cup peanuts**

In a stand mixer, blend first four ingredients well. Fold in whipped cream and spoon into Oreo crust. Swirl chocolate syrup on top and sprinkle with peanuts. Freeze.

Serves 6

PECAN PIE

½ cup melted butter

1 cup sugar

1 cup light Karo

3 beaten eggs

1 cup chopped pecans

Crust*

Whole pecans to cover the top

In a medium bowl, mix the first four ingredients together until well blended. Evenly distribute the chopped pecans on the bottom of the prebaked crust. Pour in filling. Bake at 350 degrees for 45 minutes. Once the top has set somewhat, remove the pie from the oven and place whole pecans on the top in concentric circles until the entire top is covered. Return to oven for 15 minutes or until the pie is completely cooked through. It shouldn't jiggle at all.

*Crust

1¼ cups all-purpose flour

½ teaspoon salt

1 teaspoon sugar

½ cup chilled, butter, sliced

¼ cup ice water

In a Cuisinart, blend flour, salt, and sugar. Add slices of butter and pulse until the mixture resembles meal. Add ice water and pulse only until mixture begins to ball. Turn onto pastry cloth and form into disk. Freeze until firm. Roll into a perfect round on pastry cloth. Line a fluted French 9-inch tart pan with the round of pastry. Line with parchment or waxed paper. Fill with dry beans to the top rim of the pan. Bake at 350 degrees for 30 minutes. Remove beans and paper and return to oven for about 5 minutes to dry out crust bottom. Continue with filling and baking.

Serves 6

HARVEST PIE

In the fall, other than pumpkin pie, Harvest Pie comes to mind the minute the weather cools. I love it made in 3-inch shells. The raisins make it special!

1½ cups butter

1 cup sugar

2 eggs

1 cup raisins

1 cup pecans

1 teaspoon vanilla

1 teaspoon lemon juice

Crust *see index

Melt butter and add sugar to dissolve. Remove from heat. Add remaining ingredients. Pour into prebaked crust. Bake at 350 degrees for 30-35 minutes or until set.

Serves 6

CHOCOLATE CHESS PIE

When having guests at my house, this is one of the most requested desserts I make. It doesn't need a thing, but piles of sweetened whipped cream couldn't hurt!

1⅓ sticks butter

1¼ squares unsweetened chocolate

1¼ cup sugar

¼ cup light Karo

3 eggs

⅛ teaspoon salt

½ teaspoon vanilla

Crust *see index

In a saucepan, melt butter and chocolate. Add sugar, Karo, eggs, salt, and vanilla. Pour into prebaked shell. Bake 35 minutes at 375 degrees.

Serves 6

DERBY PIE

The eternal favorite in May during Derby. However, at Thanksgiving and Christmas, I serve this pie with equal first-place cheers!

¼ cup butter

1 cup sugar

3 beaten eggs

¾ cup light Karo

¼ teaspoon salt

1 teaspoon vanilla

2 tablespoons bourbon

½ cup chocolate chips

½ cup pecans

Crust *see index

In a saucepan, melt butter. Add sugar, eggs, Karo, salt, vanilla, and bourbon. In the bottom of a prebaked crust, place chocolate chips and pecans. Pour the filling on top and bake at 375 degrees for 40-50 minutes.

Serves 6

COCONUT PIE

From the kitchen of Dianne Smith. Dianne and I have been friends for 20-something years. We met during my catering days when she headed up the Tar Heel Sports Network. She comes from a family of fabulous cooks, and we travel frequently to try great restaurants around the country. She did a cookbook some years ago honoring her mother's side of the family, Recipes from Home: The Moorefield Family Cookbook. I asked to have this recipe for my cookbook as it's my favorite coconut pie recipe. She was happy to share it!

1 stick margarine (I use butter but the original recipe calls for margarine)*

5 beaten eggs

2 cups sugar

¾ cup buttermilk

1 can coconut flakes

Crust *see index

In a saucepan, melt the margarine. Add the remaining ingredients off the heat and whisk well. Pour into the prebaked crust and bake at 350 degrees for 30 minutes or until set.

Serves 6

*Any time a recipe calls for margarine, I substitute butter. However, I will tell you what the difference is texture-wise: margarine holds things more firmly together, and butter makes things more oily. So there is an advantage to margarine, especially in cookies. I simply prefer the taste of butter. The solution I sometimes use is to use half margarine and half butter. Then the results are more consistent.

GLENWOOD CHEESECAKE

Hands down, the best cheesecake I have ever had, yes, even in New York City!

Crust:

4 tablespoons sugar

13 crushed graham crackers

10 tablespoons melted butter

In a bowl, mix ingredients together and press into a 9-inch springform pan. Bake in a preheated 350-degree oven for 10 minutes. Reduce heat to 300 degrees.

Filling:

1½ pounds softened cream cheese

1½ cups sugar

Cream together for 10 minutes in a stand mixer.

Add:

4 eggs

3 teaspoons clear vanilla

Combine with cream cheese mixture and pour into prebaked crust. Bake at 300 degrees for 1 hour. Cool for 20 minutes and top with:

Topping:

¾ **pint sour cream**

¾ **tablespoons sugar**

3 **teaspoons clear vanilla**

In a bowl, mix ingredients together and spoon onto cheesecake. Return to oven for 10 minutes.

Serves 8

ESTHER'S POUND CAKE

This is my paternal grandmother's cake. We had the exact same meal every single Sunday for lunch with a caramel cake for dessert. Her secret? Adding a little strong black coffee from breakfast to the icing. It gives the icing the richest and most delicious flavor!

1 cup butter

3 cups sugar

1 teaspoon vanilla extract

6 eggs

3 cups all purpose flour

1 cup evaporated milk (I use cream)

In a large bowl, cream butter, sugar, and extract. Beat in eggs one at a time. In a separate bowl, sift the flour. Add alternately to the butter mixture with milk. Bake in greased and floured tube pan at 325 degrees for 1¼ hours. Ice with caramel icing.

Caramel Icing:

3 cups brown sugar

¾ cup butter

8 tablespoons cream

¾ teaspoon baking powder

1 teaspoon vanilla

In a saucepan, heat sugar, butter, and cream slowly, and bring to a boil. Boil 2 minutes. Remove from heat and add baking powder and vanilla. Beat until spreadable. Be careful, it can harden quickly. Spread on cake while warm.

Serves 12

LEMON BUTTERMILK POUND CAKE

To cool a cake in a tube pan, put a glass Coke bottle on the counter. Set the hole of the hot cake pan onto the neck of the bottle, suspending the pan in the air. It not only cools quickly, but I have never had a cake stick using this method, nor have I had one fall over. When cool, flip the cake over and it will come right out. I only have Coke in bottles at my house — "It's the real thing!" And make your own lemon curd. It's easy and superior to any you can buy!

1½ cups butter

2½ cups sugar

1 teaspoon lemon extract

4 eggs

3½ cups all-purpose flour

½ teaspoon salt

½ teaspoon baking soda

1 cup buttermilk

In a large bowl, cream butter, sugar, and extract. Add eggs one at a time and beat well. In a separate bowl, sift dry ingredients. Add to butter mixture alternately with buttermilk. Bake in greased and floured tube pan at 325 degrees for 1¼ hours. Serve with lemon curd and sweetened whipped cream.

Lemon Curd:

8 ounces sugar

½ cup butter

Grated rind and juice of 2 lemons

3 beaten eggs

In a saucepan, heat sugar, butter, rind, and juice until the sugar has dissolved. Add the beaten eggs and continue stirring until the mixture thickens. Do not boil or it will curdle. Pour through a nylon sieve and chill.

Serves 12

BETSY'S CHOCOLATE CAKE

From the kitchen of Betsy Bowman. I have seen variations of this recipe my whole life. I don't know why I never tried it. It is so moist and wonderful! I had Christmas Eve dinner with the Bowmans one year and discovered this is the cake they always have. It's fabulous, and Betsy shared the recipe. It's so moist it doesn't need icing, but if you want to gild the lily . . . I say go for it!

½ cup butter

1 cup sugar

4 eggs

16 ounces Hershey's syrup

1 teaspoon vanilla

1 cup self-rising flour

In a large bowl, cream butter and sugar. Add eggs one at a time. Add syrup and vanilla. Stir in flour until blended. Bake in a greased and floured tube pan for 40-50 minutes.

Icing:

⅓ cup evaporated milk

½ cup butter

1 cup sugar

16 ounces semisweet chocolate chips

In a saucepan, bring milk, butter, and sugar to a boil. Remove from heat, add chips, and stir until melted. Pour over cooled cake.

Serves 12

WHITE CHOCOLATE BROWNIES

4 ounces white chocolate

½ cup butter

1¾ cups all-purpose flour

½ teaspoon baking powder

¼ teaspoon salt

3 eggs

1½ cups sugar

1 teaspoon vanilla

½ cup chopped pecans

In a saucepan, melt chocolate with butter. In a large bowl, sift dry ingredients. In a separate bowl, beat eggs, sugar, and vanilla. Add the melted chocolate to the egg mixture. Gradually add the flour mixture until just mixed. Fold in nuts. Pour into buttered 9-by-13-inch pan. Bake at 350 degrees for 30 minutes.

Serves 12

VANILLA ROLLED COOKIES

I have several hundred cookie cutters. You name the shape, I have it. My favorite source is H. O. Foose Tinsmithing. My cookie cutters are arranged by category in labeled plastic boxes on a huge shelf unit in my furnace room. Since I was a little girl, I have made these cookies. It is tradition for me to make them Christmas Eve, Easter, and the Fourth of July. Not to say they don't show up other times of the year, but those are definite. Christmas Eve, I use every shape, dinosaurs and cowboys and bumble bees and snowmen. The other holidays I make just the shapes that fit the day. People stand at their front door waiting for me to make a gift delivery of these delectable cookies!

3 cups all-purpose flour

1 teaspoon baking powder

½ teaspoon salt

1 cup butter

1½ cups sugar

2 beaten eggs

1½ teaspoons vanilla

In a medium bowl, sift dry ingredients. In a large bowl, cream butter and sugar. Add eggs and vanilla and mix well. Add dry ingredients. Chill until firm. Roll out thinly and cut into shapes. Bake at 400 degrees for 10 minutes. Remove from pans onto cooling racks. Ice when cooled.

Icing:

2 cups confectioners' sugar

2-4 tablespoons whole milk or half-and-half

Food coloring

In a small bowl, mix sugar with enough liquid to make an icing that will spread easily. Add colors. Ice cookies and let dry before storing.

Serves 20

CRISPY GINGER SPICE COOKIES

1 cup butter

1 cup sugar

1 egg

1 cup molasses

2 tablespoons white vinegar

5 cups all-purpose flour

1½ teaspoons baking soda

½ teaspoon salt

1 tablespoon ginger

1 teaspoon cinnamon

1 teaspoon cloves

In a large bowl, cream butter and sugar. Add egg, molasses, and vinegar. In a separate bowl, sift dry ingredients. Add to butter mixture and mix well. Chill until firm. Roll out and cut into shapes. Place on greased cookie sheets. Bake at 350 degrees for 8 minutes.

Serves 12-16

CHEWY GINGER SPICE COOKIES

¾ cup butter

1 cup sugar, plus extra for rolling cookies

2 teaspoons chopped crystallized ginger

1 egg

¼ cup molasses

2 cups all purpose flour

2 teaspoons ginger

1 teaspoon cinnamon

½ teaspoon salt

2 teaspoons baking soda

In a large bowl, cream butter, sugar, and crystallized ginger. Add egg and molasses. In a separate bowl, sift dry ingredients. Add to butter mixture and mix well. Form into balls, roll in sugar, and place on greased cookie sheets. Flatten with fingers slightly. Bake at 350 degrees for 10 minutes.

Serves 12-16

ALMOND BARS

¾ cup sugar

½ cup butter

8 ounces almond paste

3 eggs

¼ teaspoon almond extract

¼ cup flour

⅓ teaspoon baking powder

Confectioners' sugar and toasted sliced almonds for toppings

In a medium bowl, cream sugar, butter, and almond paste. Add eggs and extract. Add flour and baking powder and stir very lightly. Spoon into greased 8-inch-square pan. Bake at 350 degrees for 35-40 minutes. Top with confectioners' sugar and toasted sliced almonds.

Serves 9

IN THE MORNING

ORANGE TOAST

As a child, I alternated between Orange Toast and Cinnamon Sugar Toast every morning. On weekends we had waffles or pancakes.

½ cup butter

1 cup sugar

Grated rind of 2 oranges

Juice of 2 oranges

In a saucepan, melt butter. Add sugar, rind, and enough juice to spread well. Spread on Pepperidge Farm White Sandwich Bread. Broil until bubbly. Store in refrigerator.

Serves 8

CREPES SUZETTE

Crepes:

1 cup all-purpose flour

⅔ cup whole milk

⅔ cup water

3 eggs

¼ teaspoon salt

6 tablespoons melted butter, divided

In a large bowl, place flour. Drip in milk and water. Stir gently. Add eggs, salt, and 3 tablespoons of butter. Let rest 1 hour in refrigerator. Heat extra butter in a skillet. Use ¼ cup batter per crepe. Allow to lightly brown on first side, turn, and brown on second side.

Orange Sauce:

2 large oranges, rind and juice separated

½ cup sugar

1 cup butter

½ cup orange juice

3 tablespoons orange liqueur

Process orange rind and sugar in Cuisinart. In a saucepan, melt butter and add sugar/rind mixture. Add juice and liqueur and spoon over crepes.

Serves 8

LEMON BREAD

1 stick butter
1 cup sugar
2 eggs
Grated rind of 1 lemon
1½ cups all-purpose flour
1 teaspoon baking powder
Pinch of salt
½ cup whole milk

Glaze:
½ cup confectioners' sugar
Juice of 1 lemon

In a mixing bowl, cream butter, sugar, eggs and lemon rind. In another bowl, sift remaining three dry ingredients. Add dry ingredients to butter mixture alternately with the milk. Pour batter into a greased and floured 5-by-8-inch prepared loaf pan. Bake at 350 degrees for 45-60 minutes. Combine ingredients for glaze and pour over bread while hot.

Serves 6

PUMPKIN BREAD

Our neighbors across the street when I was little had the best live-in helper, Essie. I was devoted to her. She wasn't even our helper, but I loved her quiet manner, and she could cook — Lord, she could cook. As many meals as I could get myself invited to at the Carmichaels', I did. My mother was a great cook, but there's something about food at someone else's house that tastes special and different from the food at your own house. This is Essie's recipe, and I hope wherever she is, heaven I would guess, that she's looking down smiling that I'm still making her pumpkin bread 50 years later. My dear friend Dianne expects, yes, expects a delivery of as many loaves of pumpkin bread as I will part with on the first cool day in the fall. We have our traditions, and this is a big one. What do I get in return? I get to go to UNC football games with her. I think I'm getting the better deal, but she'd beg to differ. We also go to Bullocks for BBQ around the same day, the first cool day in the fall. If we're lucky, we do both on the same day!

3 cups sugar

4 beaten eggs

1 cup canola oil

1 pound canned pumpkin

1½ teaspoons ground cloves

1 teaspoon nutmeg

1 teaspoon cinnamon

1 teaspoon allspice

3½ cups all-purpose flour

2 teaspoons baking soda

2 teaspoons salt

⅔ cup water

In a stand mixer, mix sugar, eggs, oil, pumpkin, and spices. Sift remaining dry ingredients together and add alternately with water to the sugar mixture. Pour into a buttered Bundt pan and bake at 350 degrees for 1 hour.

SOUR CREAM COFFEE CAKE

I have always had an Easter party on Good Friday for all of my girlfriends. Living between two places and to make it easy one year, I had a brunch and served an assortment of pastries from the best European bakery in Chapel Hill. At the last moment, I was concerned about having enough, and I made this coffee cake, one of my personal favorites. At the end of the party, the platter with the croissants and other French delicacies hadn't been touched, and the sour cream coffee cake was gone and every crumb devoured. I got calls all afternoon asking if I'd share the recipe. I did, and now I share it with you!

2½ cups all-purpose flour

¾ cup sugar

1 cup brown sugar

1 teaspoon salt

¾ cup canola oil

1 beaten egg

8 ounces sour cream

1 teaspoon baking soda

1 teaspoon baking powder

1 teaspoon nutmeg

Cinnamon sugar

Icing:

¾ confectioners' sugar

2 tablespoons whole milk

In a bowl, mix flour, sugars, salt, and oil. It will be crumbly. Reserve ¾ cup of this mixture. Add to the remaining crumbly mixture the egg, sour cream, baking soda, baking powder, and nutmeg. Stir to blend. Spoon into a buttered 9-by-13-inch Pyrex. Top with reserved ¾ cup crumb mixture and sprinkle with cinnamon sugar. Bake at 350 degrees for 40 minutes. In a bowl, mix confectioners' sugar with enough milk to moisten. Drizzle over the top of the hot coffee cake.

Serves 12

SCONSET MUFFINS

1¼ cups sugar

2¼ cups all-purpose flour

1 tablespoon cinnamon

2 teaspoons baking soda

½ teaspoon salt

½ cup grated coconut

½ cup raisins

1 grated Braeburn apple

8 ounces crushed, drained pineapple

½ cup chopped pecans

2 cups grated carrots

1 cup vegetable oil

3 beaten eggs

1 teaspoon vanilla

In a large bowl, sift dry ingredients. Stir in fruits, nuts, and carrots.

In a separate bowl, whisk oil, eggs, and vanilla. Make a well in the center of the dry ingredients. Pour in oil mixture and stir gently. Mixture should be lumpy. Spoon batter into muffin liners. Bake at 350 degrees for 35 minutes.

Remove muffins from tins and cool on wire racks.

Serves 20

CINNAMON SCONES

From the kitchen of Laurie Thorp. Laurie and I met in the early '80s and worked at A Southern Season together. She has been a baker off and on in her life. These are the best I've ever had. Having lived in England, I was taught well to say "scone" that rhymes with "John," not "scone" that rhymes with "bone." Americans regularly mispronounce scone, so consider yourself schooled in the proper pronunciation. These are delicious and fail-proof and can be adapted to any flavor you wish by taking out the cinnamon and currants and adding whatever your heart desires.

5 cups all-purpose flour

1¾ cups whole wheat flour

1½ teaspoons baking soda

1½ teaspoons baking powder

¾ teaspoon salt

1½ cups chilled butter, sliced

2 cups buttermilk

¾ cup currants

Cinnamon sugar

In a large bowl, sift dry ingredients. Cut in butter. Add buttermilk and currants and stir until just mixed. Roll out on a floured pastry cloth and cut into triangles. Sprinkle with cinnamon sugar. Place on buttered cookie sheets and bake at 375 degrees for 15 minutes.

Serves 40

CHEDDAR CHIVE BISCUITS

I served these at a Halloween lunch at my house, and the guests wouldn't leave until I gave them this recipe. They are tender and leave you wanting more!

3 cups all-purpose flour

4 teaspoons baking powder

¾ teaspoon salt

½ cup butter

1 cup grated extra-sharp cheddar cheese

¼ cup chopped fresh chives

1½ cups whole milk

In a large bowl, sift dry ingredients. Cut in butter, cheddar, and chives. Add milk and mix until just combined. Roll out on floured pastry cloth and cut into shapes. Bake at 400 degrees on greased cookie sheets for 20-25 minutes.

Serves 10

BAKED EGGS

I made these most every weekend in high school. It was my mother's favorite breakfast. My father's parents kept chickens and hogs and had a very large garden, so we always had the freshest of everything. I miss going into the cellar and seeing the shelves of vegetables in Ball jars with their gem-like colors glistening as the sun hit them in the morning. My grandfather took me to the henhouse one day and told me to reach under the hen and get the eggs. I didn't want to because I thought the hen wouldn't like it. He said, "Oh no, you'll be just fine. She won't bother you." Sure enough, that hen pecked the heck out of my hand. Never again did I trust my grandfather though I continued to eat the fresh and beautiful brown eggs. You can get fresh eggs at your local farmers' market without the risk of being pecked!

Butter

4 slices lightly toasted Pepperidge Farm White Sandwich Bread

4 slices crisply cooked applewood smoked bacon

4 fresh eggs

Salt and pepper

Tabasco

In buttered ramekins, place one piece of toast torn into pieces to fit. Place one slice bacon broken in pieces on toast. Break one egg over the bacon. Salt, pepper, and add a dash of Tabasco to each ramekin. Bake at 350 degrees for 20 minutes or according to how you want your egg cooked.

Serves 4

BULL'S-EYES

This is the favorite breakfast at our house! If I dare ask what everyone wants, it's these eggs! My father grew up with fresh brown eggs every morning from the chicken coop on their property. He wouldn't eat a white egg. When I was little, our neighbor borrowed some eggs from us one day and knew my father wouldn't eat a grocery store egg, but it's all she had to repay us. So she carefully colored the return eggs with a brown crayon. I still think about her wonderful sense of humor to this day. I still buy only brown eggs to honor my father. Most people can eat more than one Bull's-Eye!!!

4 slices Pepperidge Farm White Sandwich Bread
Butter
4 fresh eggs
Salt and pepper
Tabasco
Strawberry preserves

Take each slice of bread and, using a round cookie cutter, cut out the very center of the bread. Save the holes! In a skillet, melt a tablespoon of butter and place the bread slices and the holes off to the sides. Fill the cavity in each slice with an egg and season to taste. Cook according to how you like your eggs done, turning once. Turn the holes to brown on each side. Serve the holes with preserves.

QUICHE

From start to finish, it takes about 3½ hours to make a quiche. The crust needs to be perfect and prebaked, and the bottom slightly crisp. Use only a deep French fluted tart pan. Grate your own Swiss cheese. People really will notice. On a whim last summer, I made a sausage, apple, mushroom quiche. Jack and I were the only ones working in the shop, and we prayed no one would come in so we could taste my new invention. Sure enough, wanting it got the best of us and we cut into it anyway. It immediately became our very favorite. It's the favorite of many customers, too. Try it and I think you'll love it, too!

1¼ cups cream

1¼ cup half-and-half

4 beaten eggs

Dash of Tabasco

Salt and pepper

Fresh chopped chives

6 ounces grated swiss cheese

Crust *see index

Variations:

1) Neese's Sage Sausage, apple, and mushroom
2) Spinach and feta
3) Jumbo lump crab and red bell pepper
4) Bacon and caramelized onions
5) Broccoli and red bell pepper
6) Asparagus and yellow bell pepper

In a large bowl, whisk cream, half-and-half, eggs, and seasonings. Sprinkle Swiss over the bottom of the prebaked crust. Pour the filling in carefully. Add your meat and/or vegetables. Bake at 350 degrees for 45-60 minutes or until completely set.

Serves 6

ESTHER'S WAFFLES

From the kitchen of Esther Rollins, my paternal grandmother. The waffles freeze well separated by pieces of waxed paper in freezer bags. Reheat quickly in a heated oven.

2 cups all-purpose flour
4 teaspoons baking powder
¼ teaspoon salt
2 tablespoons sugar
2 separated eggs
1¼ cups whole milk
6 tablespoons melted butter

In a large bowl, sift dry ingredients. In a separate bowl, mix yolks, milk, and melted butter. Add to dry ingredients. In a separate bowl, beat egg whites until stiff and fold into batter. Bake on buttered hot waffle iron until brown. Serve with maple syrup, fresh sliced strawberries, and sweetened whipped cream.

Serves 8

BACON, APPLE, AND MUSHROOM PANINI

2 tablespoons butter, divided

1 cup sliced button mushrooms

2 peeled, cored, and sliced Braeburn apples

8 thick slices homemade sandwich bread

12 cooked applewood smoked bacon slices

4 slices gruyere

In a skillet, melt 1 tablespoon butter and sauté mushrooms briefly. Remove mushrooms. Add another tablespoon butter and sauté apples until tender. Heat a panini pan and grill bread on one side. Add mushrooms, apples, bacon, and gruyere evenly. Top with remaining bread slices. Grill 4 sandwiches on panini grill until perfectly marked and cheese is melted.

Serves 4

RECIPE INDEX

LITTLE BITES

Brandied Fruit Mascarpone 9
Cheese Snaps 6
Corncakes 8
Cranberry Relish Butter 10
Dill Dip 12
Doo Dah Dates 7
Eleanor's Hot Cheese Dip 13
Hummus 11
Mushroom Gratin 14
Pickled Shrimp 16
Sausage and Apple Stuffed Mushrooms 15

IN A BOWL

Artichoke Bisque 25
Black Bean Soup 28
Butternut Squash and Apple Soup 20-21
Campfire Chili 34-35
Cold Cucumber Soup 19
Cream of Vidalia Soup 22
Crème Florentine 31
Eleanor's Clam Chowder 23
Fruit Gazpacho 18
Lobster Bisque 32-33
Split Pea Soup 26-27
US Senate Bean Soup 29-30
Wild Rice and Chicken Soup 24

ENTREES

Beef Bourguignon 59-60
Beek Kabobs 61
Cape Codcakes 39
Chesapeake Crab Pie 41
Chicken Curry 48-49
Corn Crepes with Shrimp and Green Chilies 42-43
Crabcakes 40
Creamy Tomato Sauce 64
East Grace Street Chicken with Spinach Fettucini 52
Eggplant Parmesan 66-67
Fried Oysters 38
Greek Chicken 50
Jekyll Island Shrimp 44
Maine Lobster Salad 47
Marinara 65
Osso Buco 56-57
Paella 45-46
Pork L'Orange 53
Raspberry Chicken 51
Ribs 54-55
Southern Diner Meatloaf 58
Spaghetti Sauce 62-63

ON THE SIDE

Baked Tomatoes 82
Black Bean Cakes 70
Bourbon Sweet Potatoes 75
Broccoli Taglierini 85
Cauliflower Gratin 77
Cinnamon Apple Salad 94
Cornucopia Salad 91-92
Cranberry Lime Sauce 93
Gingered Carrots 78
Grapefruit Salad 90
Oriental Pasta Salad 86-87
Party Potatoes 76
Pineapple Baked Beans 71
Ratatouille 80-81
Roasted Asparagus 83-84
Salad Burritos 72-73
Southern Coleslaw 89
Stuffed Acorn Squash 74
Stuffed Zucchini 79
Tabouli 88

SWEET TOOTH

Almond Bars 124
Banana Pudding 98-99
Banana's Foster 100
Betsy's Chocolate Cake 117-118
Bourbon Pralines 96
Chewy Ginger Spice Cookies 123
Chocolate Chess Pie 107

RECIPE INDEX

Coconut Pie 109-110
Crispy Ginger Spice Cookies 122
Derby Pie 108
Esther's Pound Cake 113-114
Flamed Strawberries 101
Glenwood Cheesecake 111-112
Harvest Pie 106
Lemon Buttermilk Pound Cake 115-116
Lemon Icebox Pie 102
Peanut Butter Pie 103
Pecan Pie 104-105
Vanilla Rolled Cookies 120-121
White Chocolate Bread Pudding 97
White Chocolate Brownies 119

IN THE MORNING

Bacon, Apple and Mushroom Panini 144
Baked Eggs 138-139
Bullseyes 140
Cheddar Chive Biscuits 137
Cinnamon Scones 135-136
Crepes Suzette 127-128
Esther's Waffles 143
Lemon Bread 129
Orange Toast 126
Pumpkin Bread 130-131
Quiche 141-142
Sconset Muffins 134
Sour Cream Coffeecake 132-133

EXTRAS

Beef Stock 35
Chicken Stock 51
Croutes 14
Crust 104-105

Made in the USA
Charleston, SC
29 December 2009